One equal temper of heroic hearts,
Made weak by time and fate, but strong in will
To strive, to seek, to find, and not to yield.

Sunshine in Your Pocket

SUNSHINE IN YOUR POCKET

by Denise Redford

A collection of uplifting and light-hearted poetry

First published by Olcan Press on 31st March 2020. Olcan Print/Press are a subsidiary of the Olcan Group 6 Wathem Road Dorking, W52JN, UK Email: team@olcan.co www.olcan.co

For permission contact: team@olcan.co

A CIP record of this publication is available from the British Library. First printed March 2020.

Paperback ISBN: 978-1-9160006-7-4

Foreword from the Author

As the news of the Coronavirus (COVID -19) became more intense and closer to our shores, our towns and our villages, I felt helpless and wanted to do anything I could do to help.

I have family and friends who work within the Arts across Theatre, Television and Radio. Their income and work schedules are now suddenly seriously depleted. I have put this book together with the help of Olcan and decided that 100% of the proceeds will go towards Equity's Benevolent Fund.

Thank you so much for buying this book. I hope it makes you smile and helps you to appreciate the little things in life. We are all experiencing a vast expanse of emotions at the minute but if we can keep taking one day at a time by laughing and communicating, we will get there.

Our creative industry is a sea of talented artists who bring magical escapism into our lives, which we've always loved and needed but never more so than at this present time, so I really hope this book contributes to a more stable future for someone in need.

Stay safe, stay healthy and keep that sunshine in your pocket!

All the best,

Denise Redford

Foreword from Equity

The Coronavirus epidemic is an unprecedented crisis but we will get through it by facing it together.

Thousands of entertainment workers have lost their jobs and are in dire financial need as bills are beginning to mount up. Despite the public perception, the vast majority of performers, stage managers and creative practitioners working in the entertainment industry earn modest sums and this sudden loss of income is devastating.

Equity's Benevolent Fund is here to support members with payments to help them get through this crisis. The union has put in significant funds but more is needed. If you can help this industry survive, please donate what you can.

If you are in need of help yourself, contact benfund@equity.org.uk

A little bit about the Author

For the past 40 years, I've been a former Teaching Assistant, specializing in Autism.

I live in Nottingham with Simon, my husband of 33 years. We have two older children together, Katie and Michael who both work in the Television industry. I'm also a crazy cat lady and am a doting Mum to our demanding cat Jack.

I love writing poetry and in 2018, I self-published my first book, *Just Give Me a Moment*. 100 % of the proceeds went towards the ongoing treatment of my friend's Granddaughter Ella Rose, who suffers with the life limiting condition Spinal Muscular Atrophy.

Special Acknowledgements

Thank you Katie for all of your hard work, support and dedication in enabling this book to become a reality.

Thank you to Simon for being patient regarding my strange sleeping patterns and not minding the lights being turned on in the early hours when my muse has descended!

Thank you to Michael for your constant words of encouragement.

Thank you to Olcan for publishing this and for all of the work you've provided. Team work!

Thank you to Mum, Dad and all of my friends for your endless friendship and support in all that I do.

Thank you to Jack the cat for making me take a break from writing to re-charge my batteries (well, to feed you!)

In addition, thank you to Nancy, my Nanna who saw the good in everything and always had a wise word up her sleeve.

Table of Contents

Where?

Where is my phone?

Where is my bag?

Where are the scissors

To cut off the tag?

Where are my shoes?

Where is that card?

I must be more tidy

It can't be that hard.

Where are my car keys?

Where is my coat?

What day is the dentist?

I did write a note.

Where is the note

That tells me the date?

I look at the time

Oh, is it really that late?

We need to slow down,

Gently rewind

Then all of these things

No doubt you will find.

You will find something better

At the end you will see.

You know what I found?

A healthier me!

Occasionally visit the past

But never miss the present

Life goes by so fast.

Abbreviation Nation

Where have all the old words gone?

Now it's just abbreviation.

Now "laters" T.B.H

We are the Abbreviating Nation

I'm not going for a W.L.K.

I am off for a little meander

So I won't see you anon

I'm going for a peruse and a gander.

I love the language of days gone by

When they used twenty words

Where we use four.

May I unburden your malaise and sadness

Please leave them at my door,

If it could be of our choosing

Would it not be amusing?

How would Shakespeare sound today?

And whatever your age

Continue to dream.

Colour in patterns,

Make food into faces,

Wear an old pair of shoes

And take out the laces.

Tell silly jokes,

Put on a play,

Get out the old board games

From back in the day.

All that I ask is let the memories remain,

But once in a while

Be a child again.

Nothingness

I love the nothingness that fills the air

When a snowfall blankets sound,

When technology is sleeping

There's nothingness around;

Nothingness is my favourite gentle noise.

It soothes and calms the soul.

Its other half is the noise that hurts

That fragments you as a whole,

Then daylight dawns and the world awakes

The cogs of life start turning.

Radios jolt us from our sleep,

The cat has long ceased purring,

The clinking of utensils

Microwaves are pinging.

Taps turned on

Water flows

Head is spinning, need a decision

Tension is mounting.

Are we a coffee nation?

Or afternoon tea; the new / old creation?

We buy modern mugs and cups,

We ditch the passed down China,

Then travel and pay the earth

To drink from a cup much finer.

We gasp and gaze

At a sandwich tower.

Tiny cakes a work of art,

Our lips we are licking,

Camera not clicking

The mobile recording this part.

Social media is like an Art Gallery,

Displays out pleasure and elation

The scones were to buy for

"Hashtag Tea Shop"

We will be back on another occasion.

Then somewhere in a busy commuter belt

The steam train of coffee gurgles and spits.

Cappuccino, Americano, Flat White alright

A tower of hot foam, sprinkled with bits

Where are the cafes

With plastic checked cloths?

Hands wrapped around a big mug of tea

Two bacon baps

Whilst you look at your maps,

And decide how long to the sea.

Take Me Back To Cornwall Fred

Take me back to Cornwall Fred

I really loved it there,

It really helped my asthma

All that clean fresh air.

Take me back to Cornwall Fred

Away from the dismal city.

All those tiny, white washed cottages

Narrow streets that are so pretty.

Take me back to Cornwall Fred

We could have scones and clotted cream.

We could go to Tintagel,

View the great Castle,

Life would be a dream.

Take me back to Cornwall Fred

Watch the fishermen go out to sea.

We could go there and retire

Then by the log fire,

Your grandchild could bounce on your knee.

You took me back to Cornwall Fred

To feel the summer rays.

Our holidays in Cornwall

Are now our happiest days.

Coffee Shop Confession

I said "Matt, you need to see a doctor."

"Nothing wrong with me" he replied.

I tilted my head and looked again

"It's swollen down one side!

"If you are worried or embarrassed, I can go
with you if you like?"

I warned him about the cross bar when I bought
the bike.

If you put your brakes on hard,

And your legs slip either side

You will end up with a couple of acres (and not
of land)

Hurting a lot more than your pride!

He's walking around in joggers now,

Like he's lost his horse.

He said, "You have no idea of the pain I'm in"

But I do, 'cause he's male of course.

Has he seen the doctor then?

My friend enquired

I said, "Tuesday next at four."

I will have to hide his glasses

There's a lady's name upon the door.

As I left the coffee shop

I waved my friend goodbye,

I saw Matt walking up the street

With a twinkle in his eye.

"The doctor has had a cancellation

That lady doctor she's alright.

She gave me a lot of painkilling injections,

And sixty quid for the bike!"

Matt is feeling fit and healthy now,

He's bought a racing car.

Competes in races, all over the place

He travels near and far.

I think it is quite frightening

But Matt loves the thrills.

I'm feeling shattered

My nerves in tatters

So I'm off to the docs

For some pills!

Car Boot Jumble Addiction

Can't resist going,

Can't resist knowing,

What people are selling today.

To them it is clutter

They smile when I utter

"I'll give you two pounds for that tray."

Between the colourful stalls, I wander

Heart beating faster, a little like thunder

Car Boots, Vintage Fairs, completely hypnotic

Excitement I can't measure

I root around; until I've found

My little piece of treasure.

An old book of medieval remedies

Handmade rug, old hay tractor

Posters of old Hollywood stars,

Some even signed by the Actor.

Hammers and nails,

Clothes upon rails

Old chairs, bedside table, a mirror

Books about slimming,

Lottery winning

Gadgets that help you get thinner.

Car boots to me are an Aladdin's cave

Where I can rummage and seek.

With bargains in place

A smile on my face

I'll go to another next week.

Can't resist going,

Can't resist knowing,

Just wandering around I'm content.

I'll have a meander; a really good gander

Truly a great day well spelt!

Teenage Trauma

Nail varnish on the carpet

Blonde hair round the plug

Underwear strewn

Chaotic room

Morning tea, left cold in a mug

Magazines on the bed

Opened on a fashion page

Handbags gone. She shouts

"Won't be long!"

Bed remains unmade

She has things to do

Friends to meet

Fill the hours of every day.

Buy make up, clothes, eat out

But can't save to go away

She walks through the door

Hungry once more.

Looks in the fridge and sighs

"I don't fancy that.

I don't want to get fat."

Sits and eats crackers outside

Suddenly a boy is on the scene,

A change is taking place.

The bedroom's clean

"How do you cook that Mum?"

"That smells great"

"I'm out tonight, I could be late"

I lay on the bed awake

Until I hear the door.

My body relaxes, aching for sleep

When I can worry no more

I feel that the teenager

Who was put on this earth,

To give parents a scare.

But for all the worry and grey hairs that they cause,

When they leave

You wish they were there!

No Rush Today, It's Sunday

No rush today, it's Sunday

Quality time with the world.

To a cat, every day is a Sunday

A lie in, stretched out or just curled.

No rush today it's Sunday,

We don't have to have a roast.

We could have crackers and cheese

Fly a kite in the breeze

Or spend a day at the coast.

No rush today, it's Sunday.

Think about the different religions

Or sit in the Square

With an apple and pear

And feed what's left to the pigeons.

No rush today, it's Sunday.

Get your friends over, just for a dance.

Forget getting thinner;

Have a slap up dinner,

Give a rose for a little romance.

No rush today, it's Sunday.

Just do whatever you like.

Row on the river,

Have onions with liver

Or go for a ride on your bike.

No rush today, it's Monday.

Traffic on Tuesday was bad,

Bumped the car on Wednesday,

Thursday the husband was mad,

Chips for tea on Friday.

On Saturday we told the kids to shush.

On Sunday I woke with a smile on my face

For today is the day

There's no rush!

Imagination

Faces on the curtains;

Not scary I might add.

Faces in the clouds above

Some happy, some sad.

Some have beards and funny hats,

Some stay and some move faster.

There are pictures on my wooden bench

And some resemble pasta.

I love looking for pictures

Without a moment's hesitation

It's just OK

To be this way

It's called imagination.

Tree branches look like fingers

Reaching for the sky,

A beam from the lighthouse is now what it seems

Could it be a monster with one eye?

I used to spend hours as a child

Just looking at the sky.

I thought everyone saw faces

And pictures way up high.

Now I'm getting older

It needs more concentration;

I'm just so pleased that I've been blessed

With wild imagination.

I Wish There Were Day Trips To Heaven

I wish there were day trips to Heaven

To visit the loved ones we lost.

Where would you book?

I must take a look,

How much would a trip like that cost?

If it was hundreds or thousands

I would pay it

To see those we have lost in no pain.

We would walk amongst clouds,

Mingle with crowds

Talk with our loved ones again.

I could see the earth as they see it

Travel thousands of miles in a day

I could pat all those I love on their shoulders

And whisper "Hey, Heaven's okay."

I would still be so sad to leave them again

There would never be a final goodbye.

I would book a return,

For Heaven I'd yearn

I'll see you next year in the sky.

I wish they did day trips to heaven

I am sure this is a dream of so many,

One thing is for sure,

If I could knock on God's door

The trip would be worth every penny.

Ageing With A Mission
Part I

I would love a pair of roller-skates.

I know I'm 61

I could skate to the chippy,

That would be nippy

It wouldn't take me long.

I would love to learn to paddle board.

Relaxing on still water,

I have a mate

Who paddled the lake

Lovely man who taught her.

Mind you, if I was asked to bungee jump

Oh no, I'd put up a fight!

I fancy abseiling down the wall of the chippy

As long as my harness was tight.

"Now, snorkeling I fancy"

I said to a friend

She replied, "You could go with my daughter!

Just for a laugh

I tried in the bath,

Now my ears are deaf from the water.

I will never stop my missions,

You may think that I'm a fool.

But the young folk around here

Just clap and they cheer

They think this woman is cool!

Ageing With A Mission
Part II

I had some leather trousers,

Now at the charity shop,

Menopausal when I bought them

They turned out far too hot!

I like my yoga pants

They are loose and let you move

At 61, I can move to a song

I'm keeping in the groove!

I like to walk up a big steep hill

The view at the top I would savour

I am sure that I could make it

With water and a trusty inhaler.

I love the thought of trampolining

Bouncing I adore

It would be fun

But can't be done

I've got a dodgy pelvic floor!

So I will have to stick with cycling,

And swimming at the pool.

I do Tai Chi from one 'til three

On Tuesdays as a rule.

So I'm trying to keep supple and agile

I'll let you know how it goes.

Who knows, at 71

I'll still reach down

To touch my toes!

Back To Your Roots

One day, a robot may wash your hair.

Do you think they'll say

"Would you like a magazine?"

"Are you going away?"

I think I prefer my usual girl,

She has my upmost trust.

When the robot gets near water

All their parts will rust.

Robots would be very good

At sweeping and making tea,

They won't replace Lil

She's got too much skill.

So, I don't want a robot, you see.

Supermarket Scandal

Tuesday is the big shop

That's what my parents say,

And although now in their 90's

They still like to shop this way.

Mum has the list, of all they need

Dad - he has the trolley

The shopping is placed from the front to the back

"Please don't squash the cauli."

One day not so long ago

My Mum went and lost my Dad

My Dad and the trolley had disappeared

Nowhere to be had.

I search the aisles quite frantically,

He was in the frozen aisle

I said, "Dad, why are you here?"

He pointed with a smile

"I'm following your Mum" he said

"Over there, just down the aisle."

At that point, a woman turned

And Dad looked in shock

Your Mum always wears her warm red coat

To do her weekly shop.

United with Mum in the cat food aisle

He looked at Mum in wonder

"I followed that woman

I thought she was you

Though she was a trifle younger!"

We went in the cafe

Ordered some drinks

Then Mum looked up with a smile

There was Dad's other woman

The lady in red from the aisle!

Their coats were identical

So I said "I understand but

Next time we do the Big Shop

Do it hand in hand!"

Keep Believing

Mindfulness promotes the present,

But we read our horoscope

We search for answers all day long

We follow signs of hope.

People need to have their faith

Just push away fake news.

Whatever brings us comfort,

That's what you should choose.

Believe Or Not

Inspired by Nancy's Proverbs and Superstitions

"It will be alright on the night"

Well, at the end of the day

The song says "It's hard to say I'm sorry"

That's easy for you to say.

We should not cry over spilt milk

But the cat's got the cream so we should

"There's light at the end of the tunnel

So out of bad comes good."

The darkest hour is before the dawn,

Well that's just common sense

Everyone works better in a team

So why "just sit on the fence?"

Time waits for no man

A stitch in time saves nine

What happens if there were ten stitches?

Would it create more time?

Don't run before you can walk

Would you really do just that?

You must have a great digestion

"If you can eat your hat,"

This won't get the baby bathed

"Don't mind if I do."

Take your new shoes off the table

Bad luck will come to you.

Always look on the bright side

That's the best one of them all

As most of the things that people say

Make no sense at all!

Be Still

If you want to calm yourself

And forget these daily troubles

Watch a candle flicker

Or lie in a bath of bubbles.

Go for a walk

And see with fresh eyes

The beauty beyond the front door,

New shoots are now showing

Flowers are growing

Things never noticed before.

When on the bus or in the car

We can't stop to stare

This ever changing landscape

With leaves where once was bare

When the virus leaves us,

As one day soon it will,

Will we remember the pleasure we found in standing oh so still?

I Am Not A Gadget Person

For all of those who are attempting self-assembly,

I feel your pain.

I am not a gadget person.

In fact I get perplexed

A new invention arrives on the scene

I fear what's coming next!

Especially if it arrives in parts

And you must put it together yourself

It really ought to say on the box

"Assembling is bad for your health."

I perspire looking at diagrams.

To me, it's maths again

"You must really try harder"

Is filtering my brain.

Put (A) into slot (b) and tighten (c) to click...

But purely on sight

It doesn't look right

I'm convinced at this point

I am thick.

Then I enlist the help of my Grandson

Who thoughtfully scratches his chin,

He starts to take it apart again

Then he knows where to begin.

It may have been 15 minutes later

There was a book case; secure and straight

"Gran, you needed all ten screws

And you only just used eight."

I gave him a tenner for petrol

Thankful for my bookcase conversion

I waved him off and muttered,

"I'm just not a gadget person!"

I Want To Be On TV

"Come on in" the Careers man said to me

"What would you like to be?"

"I don't want a boring job" I said

"What about TV?"

He threw back his head

Then smiled at me

"They all say that, it's true"

"There must be other things

You would really like to do.

Hairdressing, nursing, animals, shops

The choice there are many you see."

I quietly sat

Said, "I hate all that

I just want to be on TV."

I've been looking around

There's a shoe shop in town

That pays nine pounds an hour

Just think how good would that be.

I said

"I'm nobody's fool

Feet are not cool.

I just want to be on TV."

He started to fidget

And did a few sighs

Then said "You're a problem to me."

"Would you consider working with children?"

I said, "Yes, if it's on the TV."

I've decided I'm going to London,

I've got a friend you see

She's promised to show me where she works

She's rich and on the TV

I just might ask them

While I'm there

If they have any job for me.

I'll do any job

I'll make them a cob

Or do a pot of afternoon tea.

At least I'll be working in the right place

The shoe shops not for me

Then one day that careers chap

Will see me on TV.

Think

Think about the things you have

Not about what you have not,

Think about the places you've travelled

And things that you have got.

Think of all the friends you have,

Those you're yet to meet

Think of all the lovely folk

Who may live down your street.

Think of all the clothes you have

Perhaps give some away,

Think of all the food you have

A shelter needs today.

Think of all the animals

That need a forever home,

Think of those who have lost loved ones

In wars, in illness, now alone.

Also think of your body,

What it does for you,

Think of those with troubled minds

Who think their life is through;

Then think of a way you can help

To make the world much brighter

There's always something you can do

To make a heart feel lighter.

Make a cake for someone,

Buy someone homeless a meal,

One good deed is all it needs

Listen to how they feel.

Let's help everyone to swim

When they feel they're about to sink.

It really is quite easy

If we just stop and think.

Farmer Tom's Wife

"I would hate to be a farmer's wife"

I once said to my mother

I could not cope with all those smells

I couldn't touch an udder!

I would like to take those words right back,

That Summer I met Tom

I met him at the Farmers Ball.

I thought the men would pong,

We sat upon the bale of hay

The air was clear and sweet;

As Tom twirled me round the barn

I glanced down at his feet,

What did I expect to see?

Green wellies, I suppose

Denim jeans and leather boots,

Quite trendy were his clothes.

I saw more and more of Tom that summer

He had a certain country charm,

Then one day he asked me.....

Would I like to see his farm?

So, with trepidation, I rode upon his tractor

Fed the chickens too

Could I be a farmers' wife?

I began to think it through,

Then I saw it in the distance

A building like no other

It was the cowshed I could see;

Would I have to touch an udder?

"It's a really modern farm" said Tom,

"Last year, it turned to metric,

I just said "Wow"

And watched each cow get milked just by electric!"

I married Tom just two years on

I do all the baking.

Tom rises early every day

You never have to wake him.

We love the farm;

I love Tom

Country air, the healthy life,

It's all going well.

I don't notice the smell

As I love being farmer Tom's wife!

Cornershop Capers

Everyone knew the Cornershop

Just at the end of the road,

No-one saw a Councillor

They went to the shop to offload.

People shared their emotions

They would cry and laugh and shout.

They knew who died

Or who'd given birth;

Who was in prison, or out.

Rita would say

"They don't know who the father is,

It's sinful how they behave;"

Then Edna would sigh

And say "I'm not going to lie

But her Gran would turn in her grave."

"I can't cope with this damp"

I said to our Ted

"It would kill me if it gets on my chest."

My mum is the same,

With the cold and the rain,

I've nagged at her and told her to rest.

Dear, did you hear about Harry?

He's passed away

Slipped down the stairs, so they said.

His Mary is now with the butcher

It's only three weeks he's been dead.

I'll have ¼ of ham and some of that cheese

A bag of spuds, that will be fine,

I bet Ken's in the shed,

Won't enter his head

To get the washing in off the line.

So best get back,

You all take care

Are you in the Queens Head of a night?

It's getting quite bad

Richard, my lad, said every night there's a fight.

I might just carry on with the Bingo

Or swing into shape at the Club

"Get some Vick on that chest Edna

And get hubby to give it a rub."

I'm sure I'll be back

Before very long

I'll need some bits I've forgot, I am sure.

Or if you are passing by number 3

Pop in for a tea, and we can gossip some more!

A Time to Shine

Sometimes I lay awake at night,

I look up to the sky.

I ask the stars some questions

That usually start with why.

Why do we have the darkness?

Why do we have the light?

Why the sun for the day?

And moonlight for the night?

In the silence the answers come to me,

From the Universe divine;

Because each and everyone of us

Has a special time to shine.

This may look like the end, but every end has a new beginning

A word from the publisher

The words at the beginning of this publication are an ancient attempt to comfort whoever may be listening.

One equal temper of heroic hearts,
Made weak by time and fate, but strong in will
To strive, to seek, to find, and not to yield.

Two hundred years ago, Tennyson was writing during the Crimean war when scarlet fever was ripping through Victorian society. This was before the invention of the modern sewer where cholera, typhoid and smallpox were unspoken members of society. Death was a much more familiar acquaintance than it is today with infant mortality rates tens of times higher. Penicillin was one hundred years away from invention and modern medicine was non-existent.

The character speaking these words is Ulysses. Perhaps the oldest protagonist in Western Literature and the hero of the Odyssey set in ancient Greece. Once a lion of a man and a hero of the war he speaks these words in frailty - age has caught up to him. Ulysses speaks these words to an unknown listener with an unknown motive. The tone is, however, unmistakable. He is living in dark times and is struggling.

Upon returning from the Trojan War Ulysses is confronted with domestic life. You would think that after the horrors of war he would rejoice at life's quiet serenity. Ulysses doesn't see it that way. He questions how he spent his youth in battle just to see "life piled on life" back at home where "little remains." He's getting old and he looks upon his kingdom to see that discontent rules the land.

Out of this crisis, Ulysses searches for meaning. That search is something we have all experienced during the Coronavirus pandemic in 2020. Those of us who are experiencing financial issues, health issues or family disruptions know all too well the thoughts that go through your head in tough times. Fear is an uncomfortable emotion to have individually never mind collectively.

However, Ulysses speak these words as an attempt to remind himself of what is important in life. He returns to the things he finds important: his sense of community, family and solidarity. When things are uncertain, sometimes the only thing that can provide comfort are words.

I hope that this book serves the same purpose of providing an anchor in the storm. When life takes a sharp course correction, our priorities come to the surface. Family, friends, faith, community, solidarity and our search for meaning.

I hope everyone reading this is safe, healthy and comes out the other end of this difficult time with a renewed faith in society, community, health and family.

Whether the words be a poem, a call to a family member or comforting a stranger, they all have more impact than we think.

Other theatrical works from Olcan

For those actors looking for original monologues to learn for auditions or to expand their range of theatrical knowledge then look no further.

Slam Speeches

A collection of monologues by 8 female writers.

A versatile collection of monologues written by 8 writer / performers who all share one thing in common; they've all successfully written and performed their pieces at TriForce's Monologue Slam. Due to the writers being from a variety of different backgrounds, there are a vast range of perspectives for performers to explore. Between them, as both writers and performers, they have a wealth of TV, film and theatre experience and are passionate about writing monologues that not only connect with a performer but with a diverse audience too. Whether you're auditioning for Monologue Slam, drama school or for any other showcasing opportunities, this book offers a mix of heart-warming, witty and gripping speeches for you to get your teeth into.

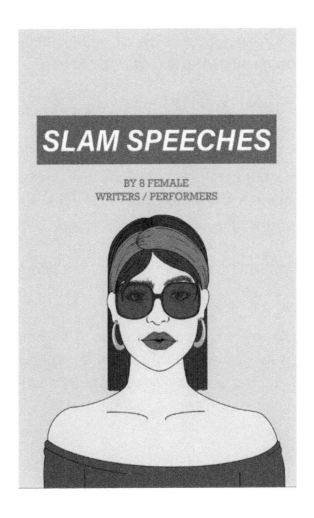

Drama School by Conor McGrath

For those students applying to drama school in the UK, Olcan publishes the #1 selling guide to auditioning and choosing the right school.

Since 2015 howtodrama.com has published free content for those aspiring actors who are applying to drama school in the UK. The head editor Conor McGrath published his complete guide in 2015 and since then it has been on the number one spot on Amazon.

"The best online resource for aspiring Actors" - Drama UK

HowtoDrama.com is dedicated to publishing content for drama school applicants, aspiring actors and those who wholeheartedly devote themselves to the craft of acting.

CONOR MCGRATH

DRAMA SCHOOL

The complete HowtoDrama
guide for aspiring Actors

Plays recently published by Olcan

Lilies and Sweets by Nathan Wright

The inaugural play from Nathan Wright was a smash hit at Pleasance and is set to return in 2020.

"Hampstead, 2015. A change meeting between two men from very different worlds leads to an uncompromising and raw friendship which challenges their understanding of love, addiction, desire, obsession, jealousy and above all companionship. After moving to London to escape a broken relationship and his drug riddled past. Al struggles to make a living and soon reverts to his old ways of dealing sweets."

A Modern Guide to Heroism and Sidekickery by Michelle Zahner

Everyone knows how superhero stories work. Save day, rescue damsel, witty one-liner, post credits scene. In a Modern Guide to Heroism and Sidekickery, Michelle Zahner brings to life a hero who doesn't want to do that. She wants to ask real questions: Why are there never pockets in lycra costumes? How do you fight a cyclone, or a rabid llama or the patriarchy? What if there's no villain? And, why don't we have a word for male damsel?

This mission combines storytelling, poetry, comedy, shadow puppetry and physical theatre with a hint of audience participation. We meet an accidental superhero, a lost journalist and a girl who doesn't need saving. This hero is really asking one thing: what do we expect from superheroes, and what would happen if we got it?

She's aware that's actually two things... She doesn't care.

"Zahner's words have a matter-of-fact poeticism to them: they captivate the mind, lift you up, play with imagery and metaphor in a most delightful manner. Her descriptions of being ordinary are so powerful you can tell they come from an honest place. And yet Zahner transforms the ordinary into something extraordinary, all via language." - Scott-Patrick Mitchell from Out in Perth.

Published by Olcan press
Part of the Olcan Group

Printed in Great Britain
by Amazon